PIKE ST.

T0057532

PIKE ST.

⊰ A PLAY ⊱

NILAJA SUN

NORTHWESTERN UNIVERSITY PRESS
EVANSTON, ILLINOIS

Northwestern University Press
www.nupress.northwestern.edu

Printed in the United States of America

10 9 8 7 6 5 4 3 2 1

LIBRARY OF CONGRESS
CATALOGING-IN-PUBLICATION DATA

Names: Sun, Nilaja, author.
Title: Pike St. : a play / Nilaja Sun.
Other titles: Pike Street
Description: Evanston, Illinois :
    Northwestern University Press, 2017. |
    "Pike St. was originally commissioned
    and produced by Epic Theatre Ensemble
    […] It had its world premiere at the
    Abrons Arts Center in New York City
    in November 2015, starring Nilaja
    Sun in all roles. The director was Ron
    Russell, with lighting design by Tyler
    Micoleau, costume design by Clint
    Ramos, set design by Mikiko Suzuki
    MacAdams, and sound design also by
    Ron Russell."
Identifiers: LCCN 2017017867 | ISBN
    9780810136250 (pbk. : alk. paper) |
    ISBN 9780810136267 (e-book)
Subjects: LCSH: Lower East Side (New
    York, N.Y.)—Drama. | Families—New
    York (State)—New York—Drama.
Classification: LCC PS3619.U495 P55
    2017 | DDC 812.6—dc23
LC record available at https://lccn.loc.gov/
    2017017867

Dedicated to Doña Lola Vasquez Vega, Candace Anderson,
and the good people of the Lower East Side

CONTENTS

PRODUCTION HISTORY

Pike St. was originally developed, commissioned, and produced by Epic Theatre Ensemble (Ron Russell, Melissa Friedman, and James Wallert, cofounders, and Robert Chelimsky, managing director) with the support of the New York State Council on the Arts. It had its world premiere at the Abrons Arts Center in New York City in November 2015, starring Nilaja Sun in all roles. The director was Ron Russell, with lighting design by Tyler Micoleau, costume design by Clint Ramos, set design by Mikiko Suzuki MacAdams, and sound design also by Ron Russell. The stage manager was Molly Minor Eustis. Since then, Sun has been touring with *Pike St.* nationally and internationally, to Washington, D.C., Minneapolis, Berkeley, and Detroit in the United States, and to Edinburgh, Scotland, and Melbourne, Australia.

PIKE ST.

CHARACTERS

CANDI

DOÑA LOLA

EVELYN

MRS. APPLEBAUM

PAPÍ

MIGDALIA

MANNY

TYKEEN

A YOUNG BOY

TEACHER

MOHAMMED

REPORTER

PRODUCTION NOTE

This play can be performed with one actor or as many as ten. The play takes place in several locations but is best staged in a fluid style with lights and sounds suggesting scene changes. The "Magic Moments" that occur in the play signify Candi's inner life, which none of the other characters in the play can see, and only she experiences.

PROLOGUE

[*Vega residence. Audience sees* CANDI, *alone in her chair, as they enter. Her body, limbs, face, and mouth are contorted. She is happily rocking, listening to the hurricane reports of NY1. Snatches from random salsa, hip-hop, Yemeni, Yiddish, and children's songs, and Navy Seal chants intersperse. We hear the sound of a drum with an Afro-Caribbean beat. Once the audience is seated,* CANDI *slowly lifts her arms up to the sky.* MAGIC MOMENT #1—*Waking. With the Afro-Caribbean beats, she claps three times and becomes . . .*]

DOÑA LOLA [*to the audience, in houselights to half*]: Come in. Come in. Come in. You feel good? You feel good?

[DOÑA LOLA *points to an audience member who may not "feel good," shakes her head, and points to herself as if to say "I got you."*]

[*She grounds herself. She does a series of breathing and clapping sequences—clapping three times and taking one deep breath in and out, beckoning the audience to join her. As the audience claps and breathes,* DOÑA LOLA *clears their energy, scoops it up above her head, walks to the open exit door, and throws their "bad" energy out the door, slamming it shut. Walking back to the stage, she claps three times. She takes*] one last deep breath, smiles while exhaling sweetly, and peeks at the audience . . .]

You feel good? Ah! You feel good! You look good. *Gracia a Dios!* Thank You, God. Thank You, God. Thank You . . .

[*With a grand gesture, perhaps a clap or a stomp, we hear* EVELYN . . .]

SCENE 1

EVELYN: Pike Street. Sixty Pike Street. One-zero-zero-zero-two. Under the Manhattan Bridge? Uh, next to what used to be Pathmark? Yeah . . . well, I am calling because I have life-sustaining equipment in my home and I need to know if we're gonna have electricity issues today and . . . Yes, I know you are very busy this morning, but . . . Yes, I know you are not God. Yes, I was supposed to preregister with a doctor. Respirator, home dialysis machine, generator . . . Yes, I'll hold. Ugh.

[CANDI *chuckles.*]

[*To* CANDI] Good morning, Candi. You laughing at your *mami?* Well, wake up because we have a very tight schedule today. [*On the phone*] Yes, I'm still here. OK. [*To* CANDI] Candiiiii? Candi Candi Candi Candi Candiiiii? Remember when you were ten and had dance, karate, theater, student government, S.A.T. classes? Who goes to S.A.T. classes at ten? "Gotta keep that tight schedule." [*Lighting candles*] Benevolent Virgin Mary, mother of God, *Santa María, Madre de Dios*, we thank you for this morning. This good good good . . .

[*The doorbell rings.*]

MRS. APPLEBAUM: Good morning.

EVELYN [*opening door*]: Mrs. Applebaum! Good morning! Come in, I'm on the phone with Con Ed.

MRS. APPLEBAUM: Oy, Con Ed. No, no, no, I just wanted to see my little girl.

EVELYN: Little? She's fifteen. [*On phone*] Yes, I'll hold. [*To* MRS. APPLEBAUM] There's gonna be a hurricane today, Mrs. Applebaum. Do you have D batteries?

MRS. APPLEBAUM: Hurricane? Oy! I lived through the Depression! We had nothing barely but the shoes on our feet! And, we did it without the help of double Ds.

EVELYN: D batteries, Mrs. Applebaum. Just D.

MRS. APPLEBAUM: We lived on family, water, a little food, and a whole lot of love.

[MRS. APPLEBAUM *looks at* CANDI.]

Isn't that right, my girl?

EVELYN: She's not your girl, Mrs. Applebaum.

MRS. APPLEBAUM: . . . Are you Puerto Rican?

EVELYN: Pardon?

MRS. APPLEBAUM: Are you, er, Puerto Rican?

EVELYN: Ah, here we go again. Yes, Mrs. Applebaum, I am Puerto Rican.

MRS. APPLEBAUM: Ah, welcome to America!

[MRS. APPLEBAUM *hugs* EVELYN.]

EVELYN: Thank you, I was born here.

MRS. APPLEBAUM: You're the third Puerto Rican I've met. There's Mrs. Rivera from the laundry and José the bag boy at the grocery downstairs. Very handsome. And now you! Three's a lucky number.

EVELYN: It certainly is. It's nice to meet you. I'm Evelyn Lola Vega.

MRS. APPLEBAUM: I'm Gloria Elaine Applebaum. My husband downstairs is Bruce and we have a little girl too. Her name is Rachel. She's your age. [*Whispering, referring to her daughter and* CANDI] Maybe they could play sometime? I'm very open-minded.

EVELYN: I see that.

MRS. APPLEBAUM: Does she er. . . speak?

EVELYN: She's uh . . . shy.

MRS. APPLEBAUM: Oh, she's shy! What's her name?

EVELYN [*on phone*]: Yes, I'm still here. [*Speaking slowly, as if to spell it out*] Respirator, home dialysis machine, genera— Yes, I'll hold. [*To* MRS. APPLEBAUM] Candace. But, we call her Candi for short.

MRS. APPLEBAUM [*loudly*]: Hello, Candi! You have such a pretty smile. *Shayna punim,* my girl! *Shayna punim.* We're gonna be the best of friends. [*To* EVELYN] Have you been reading the paper, watching the news?

EVELYN: Yes, I have, the storm is going to be—

MRS. APPLEBAUM [*interrupting*]: That Martin Luther King fella's really making headlines.

EVELYN: . . . Mrs. Applebaum?

MRS. APPLEBAUM: Yes?

EVELYN: Martin Luther King . . . has been dead for some time now.

MRS. APPLEBAUM [*gasping*]: Cancer?

EVELYN: Yeah.

MRS. APPLEBAUM [*almost in tears*]: Oh, what a shame!

EVELYN: Tell me about it. . . . I'm going to the store. I can pick you up some batteries just in case. Need anything else? Food, milk, bialys from Kossar's?

MRS. APPLEBAUM: That's not too far for you?

EVELYN: I'll get Manny to pick them up.

MRS. APPLEBAUM: Manny's coming home? Mazel tov. He hasn't been home in thirteen months and five days!

EVELYN: That, you remember.

MRS. APPLEBAUM: But it's all the way on Grand. He'll have to take Pike to East Broadway, then turn on Essex past the pickle stand on the left. Tell him to take a moment to smell the pickles. There's nothing like the smell of pickles on Essex.

EVELYN: For you, anything.

MRS. APPLEBAUM: Oy, then I'll take three bialys, five onion bagels, seven mini pletzels, a fire extinguisher . . . What? I may not have my wits about me, but I'm no fool.

EVELYN: Never the fool! Good-bye, Mrs. Applebaum.

MRS. APPLEBAUM [*exiting*]: Welcome to America!

EVELYN: I was born right in this apartment. You helped deliver me and called me Little Buddha because of the red dot on my forehead. Be careful walking . . . down . . . the . . . stairs. [*On phone*] Hello, yes I am so sorry. OK, thank you. Ten minutes? OK, I'll be waiting.

PAPÍ [*peeking through bedroom door*]: Is she gone?

EVELYN: Yes, Papí, she's gone.

PAPÍ: Oh my God, *esa judía!*

EVELYN: Um, Papí, is it possible to not start every morning with racism?

PAPÍ: You think they see me and they say, "That's a man"? No! They say, "That's a spic!"

EVELYN [*singing*]: Good morning, I don't want Candi to hear your negativity. Good morning, good morning to you!

PAPÍ: Negativity? Ugh! [*Yelling down the stairs*] And I lived in the Depression too. . . . But it was the nineteen eighties and his name was Ronald Reagan.

EVELYN [*still singing*]: Does every morning have to start so political? Lift up the tone of your voice. PLEASE?

PAPÍ: Candi? Pssh . . . she can't hear.

EVELYN: Yes, but she can feel the vibrations of anger and resentment. Start her day off right for once, please.

PAPÍ [*to* CANDI]: *Mira,* Candi. Don't listen to your *mamí,* OK? Toughen up! We have plenty of men like you in the VA, and you know what they do? Ah? Ah? Ah?

EVELYN: What do they do, Papí?

PAPÍ: They . . . they . . . they . . .

EVELYN: . . . fart in a coffee cup . . .

PAPÍ: Fart in a coffee cup . . . to clean . . . their dentures!

[PAPÍ *laughs and pops his dentures in.*]

See? See? I start with a joke. I lift up my voice. My *polquería* voice.

EVELYN: Thank you, Papí, for trying. Even though she can also feel the vibration of *sarcasm,* which is a very low vibration.

PAPÍ: Ugh, give it a rest. *¿Y dónde está mi café?*

EVELYN: Ay, I'm sorry. Your coffee. I was doing the tango with Con Edison.

PAPÍ: Let me tell you, we New Yorkers are some dumb motherfuckers to pay every month a company that starts with the word CON. *Dame* high five for that one!

EVELYN: Papí, I don't have time to be high-fiving you today. We're on a very tight schedule. Milk?

PAPÍ: Don't put that soy sauce in *mi café*!

EVELYN: Soy milk, Papí. And I'm sorry we don't have the mucus of a fatty cow's rancid teats this morning.

PAPÍ: Be careful! [*Pointing to* CANDI] She understands sarcasm. . . . *¿Y mi* Post? *¿Mi* Daily News?

EVELYN: There *y* there.

[PAPÍ *drinks and he reads.*]

PAPÍ: Ugh. Storm *ni* storm. Look, it's just drizzling and the lucky tree outside is not even eswaying *tampoco*. In Puerto Rico, we know about hurricanes. Storm *ni* storm.

[*He reads.*]

Put out his article so it can be the first thing he sees.

EVELYN: It's right here. [*Pointing to it*] And, I taped his story on Fox. He looks good. Healthy.

PAPÍ: Too skinny, if you ask me, *pero* . . .

[*He reads.*]

. . . Prieta, you have class today?

EVELYN: Yes, one. Online.

PAPÍ: One line?

EVELYN: *Online.* In the computer.

PAPÍ: Ah. . . . But who goes to school for—

EVELYN: I do, Papí, because we need to make money somehow, and energy healing is very popular nowadays.

[PAPÍ *thinks for a beat.*]

PAPÍ: Energy healing, ugh. Your mother, Doña Lola Vasquez . . .

EVELYN: Doña Lola Vasquez . . .

PAPÍ: Lola Vasquez Vega healed everyone in Loisaida with her bare hands. She did not go to school for that. GOD gives you that. Pay GOD. Not some white man.

EVELYN: Papí, please, I don't pay a white man. [*Thinking*] I pay a white lady.

PAPÍ: Manny has money. He'll be getting paid.

EVELYN: I'm not going to take Manny's money. He fought for that. Besides, you're the man of the house. And you're gonna tell him about the *botánica.*

PAPÍ: And what does that mean?

[EVELYN *sighs.*]

[*Mocking her sigh and finishing his coffee*]: Ew! Soy sauce. OK! Migdalia is coming over in a few minutes, and you know what that means?

[*He whistles;* EVELYN *is clueless.*]

I'm going to need the place to myself.

[PAPí *whistles louder;* EVELYN *is dumbfounded.*]

You know? [*Lifting his eyebrows*] You know? Nooky, nooky.

EVELYN: Oh God, Dad, please. I'm gonna vomit in my mouth. Look, I'll take a walk to the Duane Reade on Delancey, and then I'm coming right back. I'm giving you forty minutes. *Quarenta minutos. Y no más.* I need to buy candles.

PAPí: More candles? It's like a memorial to Jimmy Hoffa in here.

[*He laughs.*]

EVELYN [*mocking laughter*]: Did Jimmy Hoffa even have a funeral?

PAPí: I don't know, it was the nineteen eighties. The Great Depression.

[*Phone rings.*]

EVELYN [*answering the phone*]: Yes. Yes. Yes. This is Evelyn. Uh, no. No, no, no, we're not going to a shelter. Why? Well, we went to the one at Seward Park the last time it was the "storm of the century," and the generators were old and tapped out. By the third day, all the hipsters wanted to charge their laptops and cell phones on the same outlet as my daughter's dialysis, and then we gotta deal with all the kids screaming, "Mommy, Mommy, what's the matter with that girl? What's the matter with that girl?" And then, all the neighbors I haven't seen in years with eyes of sympathy—"Oh my God, I was so sorry to hear." "She was the smartest girl in the neighborhood." "You still don't know what she has? What mother in this day and age doesn't know what disease, what crippling disease her daughter has? And, how's Manny?" All those bitches, all they care about is "How's Manny? Coming back home? I saw him on TV. He's our heroooo." Then my *papí* is flirting with anything with a vagina. I mean, I don't let it bother *me*, but *she, she* feels the feelings of others and it swallows *her*, so it's just less stress for everyone if we stay home. [*Embarrassed for venting*] Besides, we can't bring her chair down five flights.

PAPí: Tell them the elevator's broke.

EVELYN: The elevator's broke . . . N. Broken. Yes, I'll hold. [*To herself*] *Ay mi madre.*

PAPí: *Calmate muchacha.* "Con Edison. We're a CON!" *Dame* high five. [*She doesn't.*] Candi? [*Turning to* CANDI] Give *abuelo* high five. [*Negotiating with her hand*] *¡Así eso!*

EVELYN: Stop. Stop. Stop.

PAPí: What? Take it easy. Take it easy. You too tense. That's why Ramon's not around anymore. *Pendejo.* You need a real man in your life already. Which reminds me . . . I gotta get ready. Nooky, nooky.

[*He whistles off.*]

EVELYN [*on phone*]: Yes. It's me, my daughter, my father . . . and my brother. My baby brother is coming home today.

SCENE 2

[MAGIC MOMENT #2—*Mom therapy. We hear meditative flute music.* CANDI, *in her mind, dances like a limber ballerina, lifting one arm at a time to the sky. She is happy, she is free. In an instant, she sits in her chair, her body, limbs, and face contorted as in scene 1.* EVELYN *helps* CANDI *lift her arms, one at a time.*]

EVELYN: That's it, Candi. Feel the energy flow up and down. Up and down. The energy from the divine. The energy from earth. Pacha Mama—your angels, your spirit animals. "I live in the heart of God. I am loved. I live in the heart of God. I am healed. I live in the—

[*The doorbell rings.*]

HEART OF GOD! I AM [*calmly, to* CANDI] at peace, peace, peace." Keep praying, *mamita.* Breathing in wind spirit through your aura. *Om namah shivaya, Om namah shivaya, Om namah . . .*

[CANDI *chuckles.* EVELYN *opens the door. It is* MIGDALIA.]

MIGDALIA: *Buenos días.*

EVELYN: Good morning, Migdalia.

MIGDALIA: Your father told me you were . . .

EVELYN: Just leaving, yes. Candi was doing her stretching.

MIGDALIA: Ah, she can estrech?

EVELYN: Yes, like Pina Bausch.

MIGDALIA: Is that a fruit? . . . *¿Y qué heto?*

EVELYN: That? Oh, it's a generator in case we lose power. I just don't know how it works yet.

MIGDALIA: Just go to a shelter.

[*Beat.*]

EVELYN: It was nice to see you again, Migdalia. I'm going to Delancey. Need anything?

MIGDALIA: From Delancey? No! What am I, an immigrant?

EVELYN: Yes, yes, you are actually.

MIGDALIA: Yes, but I don't look like one.

[*Beat.*]

EVELYN: Candi loves NY1. Please keep the TV on NY1, OK? It has to be NY1. Nothing else. No *novelas*, no *¿Quién Tiene La Razón?*, and please, please no *Price Is Right*. It'll get her all . . . all . . . *agitao*.

MIGDALIA [*correcting her*]: *Agitada.*

EVELYN: *Agitada.*

MIGDALIA: Ay, well excuse me, Candi, such requirements. I'm just here to see your *abuelo*. You're very tense, you know, Evelyn?

EVELYN: Really? Cuz I feel as cool as a cucumber today. Good-bye, Princesa Candi, or should I call you Eagle Standing Fish? [*To* MIGDALIA] Good-bye, Migdalia. *Bendición*, Migdalia.

MIGDALIA [*laughing*]: Ay, I'm not old enough to give *bendiciones pero que Dios te bendiga.*

EVELYN: And could you put the cigarette . . . out? Thank you.

[*She leaves slowly, eyeballing* MIGDALIA*'s cigarette.* MIGDALIA *pretends to look for an ashtray, waits for* EVELYN *to leave, and takes a long drag.*]

MIGDALIA [*mocking* EVELYN]: Thank you. "Princesa Standing Fish" [*blowing smoke in* CANDI*'s face*], do you mind?

[MIGDALIA *changes the channel to* The Price Is Right.]

That's easy. Nineteen. Nineteen dollars. Nineteen!!!

PAPÍ [*whistling and singing*]: *Usted abusó . . .*

MIGDALIA: Nineteen!

PAPÍ [*singing*]: *Sacó un provecho de mí, abusó.*

MIGDALIA: Nineteen. *¡Coño!* Why do you not say nineteen?

PAPÍ [*singing*]: *Sacó un partido de mí, abusó . . .*

MIGDALIA: *¡Idiota!*

PAPÍ [*singing*]: *De mi cariño, usted abusó . . .*

[CANDI *is starting to become uncomfortable with the sounds of* The Price Is Right.]

MIGDALIA: Is that my handsome George Clooney?

PAPÍ: Is that my sexy Sophia Loren?

MIGDALIA: Sophia Loren? I'm not old enough to know who that is, *pero . . .*

PAPÍ: Ay, Miggie. I feel like I haven't seen you in years.

[*They kiss.*]

You miss me?

MIGDALIA: Of course, I miss you.

[*They kiss.*]

Are you ready for the rain? You have D batteries?

PAPÍ: No, but I see two double Ds in front of me that could light my way to a rainbow.

[*They kiss.*]

MIGDALIA: Ay, I feel faaaaat.

PAPÍ: Just how I like it.

MIGDALIA: Papí, no. I need new lingerie, but I can't afford . . .

PAPÍ: How's twenty?

MIGDALIA: Twenty?! For lingerie? What am I?

PAPÍ: Twenty-five?

MIGDALIA: Sixty dollars.

PAPÍ: Sixty! What you doing to me, *mujer*?

MIGDALIA: I'll make it worth your while.

[*Beat. He pulls her away from* CANDI.]

PAPÍ [*whispering*]: You gonna do the thing?

MIGDALIA: I'm gonna do the thing.

PAPÍ: Ooh, I love it when you do the thing! OK, *sesenta peso*, here. Sixty. [*Thinking*] Zero-six-zero, atsa good number. . . . You love me?

MIGDALIA: Once I get that lingerie, you gonna see how much I love you!

PAPÍ: OK, *pero*, last time I gave you money, I never saw the goods.

MIGDALIA: You want good. I give you good.

[MIGDALIA *sexily walks into the bedroom.*]

PAPÍ: Oof! Candi, I'm going into the room to bake some cookies, to dip the gravy boat, to um . . . butter the muffin. Mamí will be back soon, then Manny comes home!

[PAPÍ *exits.*]

[MAGIC MOMENT #3—*Crazy scary* Price Is Right *music is heard.* CANDI *starts to hyperventilate. She, in her mind, is trying to block her body from invisible punches. She is left panting from the song and sounds of the audience clapping.*]

SCENE 3

MANNY [*slowly walking in*]: I'm home! Candi! Candi?

[CANDI *is still panting.* MANNY, *recognizing this symptom, searches for the remote. He changes the channel to NY1. She calms down and breathes regularly, as before.*]

Much better, ah? You look good.

[MANNY *looks around the house. He shuffles through the* Daily News *until he finds "his" page.*]

I look good.

[*He lights a candle.*]

Our Father, Who art in heaven. Thank you for getting me home safely, that my plane did not go into the Atlantic, and that I kicked some major *ass*!

[*Beat.*]

Candi? Feel better? You look good, *mamita.* Where's everyone? Evelyn? PAPÍ?

MIGDALIA [*offstage*]: *Ay, mi madre. Ay, mi madre. ¡Ay, mi madre!*

MANNY: Papí?

PAPÍ [*offstage*]: *¡Jesu Cristo!*

MANNY: Papí?

[*Beat.*]

PAPÍ [*offstage*]: Manny? That you?

MANNY: Uh, yeah.

PAPÍ [*swinging the door open*]: Manny!

MANNY: Papí!

PAPÍ: Manny!

[*They hug each other tightly.*]

MANNY: *¡Bendición!*

PAPÍ: *¡Que Dios te bendiga!*

MANNY: I missed you!

PAPÍ: I missed you too!

MANNY: I have so many stories to tell!

PAPÍ: I want to hear them all!

MANNY: Papí, let me ask you a question.

PAPÍ: Anything, my son.

MANNY: Are you butt naked right now?

PAPÍ: *¡Ay a diatre, mi pantalones!*

[PAPÍ *pulls his pants up.*]

Manny!

MANNY: Papí!

[*They hug again.*]

Where's Evelyn? I came home. *The Price Is Right* was on, and Candi was all . . . all . . . *agitada.*

PAPÍ: *Agitao.*

MANNY: *Agitao.*

PAPÍ: She went to get candles.

MANNY: More candles? It's like Whitney Houston's funeral up in here.

MIGDALIA [*sultrily*]: ¡*Buenos días!*

MANNY: Oh. Hello, I'm Manuel.

MIGDALIA [*chuckling*]: Migdalia.

MANNY [*whispering*]: Papí, who's that?

PAPÍ [*whispering*]: We'll talk.

MIGDALIA: *Bueno, guapo.* Call me later.

MANNY: It was a pleasure.

MIGDALIA: Oh, no. The pleasure was all mine.

[*She salutes* MANNY *sexily, kisses* PAPÍ, *and exits.*]

PAPÍ: Be careful . . . walking down . . . the stairs . . .

[PAPÍ *closes the door.*]

Why you home so early? We don't expect you till two.

MANNY: I took an early plane cuz of the storm.

PAPÍ: Ay storm *ni* storm.

[PAPÍ *looks him over.*]

How's my favorite Navy Seal?

MANNY: Been farting hummus for the last eighteen hours, but I'm glad to be home, Papí.

PAPÍ: Your *mamí* would be so proud! Come on, let's have a drink.

MANNY: No, Papí. I don't hardly drink no more.

PAPÍ: What! Come on. Come on. One drink.

MANNY: Nah nah nah nah nah.

PAPÍ: Ah ah ah ah ah. You just kicked some Taliban ass and you won't have one drink with your father? In my house? *Dame un break-e.*

MANNY: OK. OK. One . . . shot . . . of . . . rum.

PAPÍ: That's . . . all . . . we . . . need.

[*He pours two shots.*]

Salud!

[*They drink.*]

OOF! Let's get this party started. ¡*Música!*

MANNY: None of that old sad *guitarra*, Papí.

PAPÍ: *Ay pero qué gringo tú eres.*

[*He thinks.*]

I know! I know! Blast from the past! AAAAH!

[*He puts on "Rapper's Delight" by the Sugarhill Gang.*]

MANNY: AAAAH!

PAPí: Remember your first crush. What was her name? That *morenita.*

MANNY: Aisha.

PAPí: You LOVED her.

MANNY: I learned all the lyrics just for her and did the entire song in front of the whole school. [*Singing*] *I said a hip hop . . .*

PAPí: —*rock it to the bang . . . of the boogie the beat!* AAAAAHHHHH! [*They high five.*] I bet you got laid real good that night.

MANNY: Papí, I was ten.

PAPí: I know. I know. Late bloomer. *Bendito.* One more. One more. Come on, long flight.

MANNY: Just *one* more.

PAPí: *Aha.* One for you, two for me. *¡Salud!*

MANNY: *¡Salud!* To love.

[*They drink.*]

PAPí: *Salud.* Come on, Candi. *Salud. Salud.*

[*He claps.*]

OK. Time for some real music.

[PAPÍ *puts on "Oye Cómo Va" by Tito Puente. He dances passionately.*]

MANNY: You look good, Papí.

PAPÍ: I feel good. I feel good. I feel real good. But, for the record, this aging business is not what it's cracked up to be. Don't do it.

MANNY: Really? So, what's your secret?

PAPÍ: You see that Migdalia. She's a fox, no?

MANNY: Yeah, she's hot.

PAPÍ: Cuz she don't think I'm old. See life, it's about *being*, not thinking. I don't think I'm old. I just be . . . young. I don't think I'm sick. I just be OK. I don't think I'm broke. I just be . . . I just be . . .

MANNY: Rich, Papí?

PAPÍ: I didn't play my numbers today.

MANNY: That's not like you, Papí.

PAPÍ: It's that Migdalia. She makes me all . . . all . . . what's the word?

MANNY: Forgetful?

PAPÍ: I don't know. I forgot.

MANNY: Is that Evelyn?

[EVELYN *walks in, with bags.*]

EVELYN: Manny!

MANNY: Evelinda!

EVELYN: You're home early. Papí, Papí, Papí take my bags so I can say hi to my bro-bro. Manito! Our hero!

[*She hears the music playing.*]

Let me put on some real music.

[EVELYN *puts on "Set It Off" by Strafe. They hug and dance.*]

MANNY: Evelyn! You look good . . . you look *thin*.

EVELYN: I know. I'm not eating sugar.

MANNY: Good for you! I'm off caffeine.

EVELYN: I did that last year. It will change your life.

MANNY: Eating dairy?

EVELYN: No dairy, rice, pasta, potatoes, bread. I already lost ten pounds.

MANNY: No coffee and my skin cleared up like [*snapping his fingers*] that.

[PAPÍ *shuts off the music.*]

PAPÍ: Well, *fíjate*, I smoke, drink, fuck, shit, eat *cuchifritos*, and I look better than the both of you put together. One more, come on. Ev!

EVELYN: No! I have a class in thirty minutes.

MANNY: Energy healing?

EVELYN: You know it!

MANNY: Mamí would be so proud. It's very popular these days, Papí. How's the *botánica*?

PAPÍ: Well . . .

EVELYN [*avoiding*]: We'll talk about that later. . . . Manny, lemme ask you, do all the women over there wear those things over their faces?

MANNY: Yeah. Most of them.

EVELYN: Wow! Cuz I could really use one for those days that I look like shit.

MANNY: Damn, Evelyn. That's pretty racist.

PAPÍ: No! It's not really racism if they're not around to hear it. Welcome home, my son!

[*They drink.* PAPÍ *plays "Black Magic Woman" by Carlos Santana.*]

EVELYN: Manito, do me a favor before it gets bad out there, could you get Mrs. Applebaum a fire extinguisher and . . .

MANNY: . . . her bialys?

EVELYN: Psychic!

MANNY: No, wait, wait, lemme guess. She wants me to take East Broadway to Essex and take a moment to smell the pickles.

EVELYN: Witchcraft!

MANNY: *¡Jugilanga!*

PAPÍ: You two laugh. But that ain't funny. There's a fine line between good magic and bad magic. Manito, do me a favor and play my numbers at the spot on Grand. You remember them?

MANNY: Of course. Zero-six-zero, five-three-three, one-one-five, one-one-six, and four-eleven combo!

PAPÍ: He is really an American hero. *¡WEPA!*

[*Sound of an intercom buzzing.*]

MANNY [*looking out the window and opening it*]: Tykeen! Tykeen! . . . Yeah, just now. Whatchu up to? Wanna walk to Grand? . . . A'ight. Meet me across the street in the park. [*To* PAPÍ *and* EVELYN] I'm gonna get a slice with Tykeen. Anybody want anything?

EVELYN: Get Candi some hot chocolate and Ritz crackers.

[*She winks at* CANDI.]

PAPÍ: As for me, get me an *arroz con pollo* from the Dominican place, an egg foo yong from the Chinese place, a rugelach from the Jewish place, and my numbers from the Arabs.

MANNY: Got it! Phew, I'm a little toasted.

PAPÍ: Take one more. For the road. Evelyn, get your glass of water. *¡Salud!* Come on, Candi. To the storm!

MANNY AND EVELYN: To the storm!

[MAGIC MOMENT #4—*Spotlight on* CANDI. *She listens happily to the music in her chair. The music shifts and we see her, in her mind, pop out of her chair and play a jamming air guitar. Winking and smiling at the audience. Rocking out, like Carlos Santana. The music shifts and she is back in her chair, listening happily as before.*]

SCENE 4

[*Coleman Square Park.*]

MANNY: Tykeen Wong Chang!

TYKEEN: Yo! Look at you. Dwayne the Rock Johnson up in here.

MANNY: Yeah, you know you know. Gotta stay in shape.

TYKEEN: It looks good on you, bro. I'm fat as fuck. How's the family?

MANNY: Crazy as always.

TYKEEN: And Candace? She, uh . . . she, uh . . . ?

MANNY: You know Evelyn, always hoping. One day at a time, right?

TYKEEN: It's amazing how life can change in a moment.

MANNY: In an instant. [*Snapping his fingers*] Just like that!

TYKEEN [*snapping his fingers*]: Just like that! [*He looks around.*] Yo, you wanna smoke this joint right quick?

MANNY: Um, damn, you know . . . I haven't eaten yet and I got about four shots of rum in me.

TYKEEN [*lighting up*]: Your father's rum? . . . Last time I drank your father's rum [*puffing*] I woke up in some strange lady's bed [*puffing*] with two dollars in my pocket [*puffing*], a tooth missing [*puffing*], and cat hair in my mouth.

[*He exhales.*]

MANNY: Yeah, I'm surprised he's still alive . . . Smells nice. Aah, I'll take a little.

TYKEEN [*laughing and passing the joint*]: A'ight!

[MANNY *smokes.*]

MANNY [*coughing and choking*]: This some new stuff?

TYKEEN [*proudly*]: Yeah . . .

[*His phone rings. He looks at the caller ID and rolls his eyes. He picks up.*]

Mah, Mah! Why are you calling me? I just left the building two minutes ago. *Hmm hai, aw hmm hai sick gun yeen-ah. Hoe! Hoe! Joy qin-ah!* All right, all right!

[*He hangs up.*]

My moms is trippin'. Yo! Tell me about them Al-Qaeda chicks. Betchu they nice.

MANNY: I guess.

TYKEEN: Yeah, nice and . . . [*To a female passerby*] Hello, gorgeous? GORGEOUS! I could talk to you. I could talk to you? Oh, I see. You hurrying. Hurrying . . . for a hurri-cane? God bless you. [*To* MANNY] Yeah, Al-Qaeda chicks. Nice and quiet. Not like these argumentative bitches around here.

MANNY: How's Aisha?

TYKEEN: Yo, I ain't seen'd her in a minute. Moved back to Georgia with her moms.

MANNY: Really? And Destiny?

TYKEEN: Destiny with her too.

MANNY: How old is she now?

TYKEEN: Destiny? Four. Yo, check it.

[TYKEEN *shows* MANNY *pics on his phone.*]

She was Princess Tiana, Cinderella, and SpongeBob for her birthday. Aisha made her rotating outfits. Worked on them for a month. All my idea.

MANNY: Damn.

TYKEEN: And then I designed this whole pink and green space odyssey with dinosaurs [*puffing*], pictures of hairless kittens on the walls [*puffing*], and statues of old leaders from the Ottoman Empire.

Them four-year-olds' minds was blown.

[*He exhales.*]

MANNY: I bet you they were. You and Aisha always were good at design.

TYKEEN: Yeah, yeah. You know. You know. I still got it in me.

[*He chuckles.*]

[*Beat.*]

MANNY: So, why'd she leave?

TYKEEN: She said I was emotionally abusive.

MANNY [*perks up, attempting to hide his anger*]: Were you?

TYKEEN: Who isn't emotionally abusive in New York City? With every year you live here, you graduate to the next level of abusiveness. Emotionally abusive, check. Verbally abusive, check. You become mayor—politically abusive, check. [*Puffing*] You get old and find Jesus—spiritually abusive [*exhaling*], . . . check.

MANNY: Still, Aisha was one of the good ones. You should . . .

TYKEEN: Damn I'd love to meet one of them Taliban hotties. [*To another female passerby*] Hello, gorgeous? GORGEOUS! I could talk to you. I could talk to you. Oh, I got you. I got you. You hurrying. Hurrying . . . for a hurri-cane. God bless you. [*To* MANNY] I'd love to meet one of them Taliban hotties. I know they love you. Ooh, you one lucky ass nigga!

[*Lightning strikes.* MANNY *grabs* TYKEEN *by the collar and lifts him up angrily.*]

MANNY: Who you calling nigga, soldier?!!! I'm Puerto Rican!!! I saved your life!!!

TYKEEN: Yo, chill!

MANNY: You better recognize rank when it's talking to you!

TYKEEN: Yo, Manny. Easy, easy.

MANNY: I saved your life, soldier!

TYKEEN: Yo, Manny, wake the fuck up!

MANNY [*snapping out of it*]: Ty, where are we right now?

TYKEEN: Um, Coleman Square Park?

MANNY: And, what is that noise over our heads?

TYKEEN: The B train going over the Manhattan Bridge? Manny, are you all right?

MANNY: Yeah.

TYKEEN: You wanna let me go, or . . .

MANNY: Oh yeah.

[MANNY *releases* TYKEEN *from his grip.*]

TYKEEN [*coughing*]: I think we need some food in our bellies.

MANNY [*lost in thought*]: Yeah, yeah. Jet lag.

YOUNG BOY [*running up to them*]: Mista!

MANNY: Yo, put that away.

YOUNG BOY: Mista!

MANNY: Put the smoke away, Ty.

TYKEEN: What? Damn.

[*He takes three quick puffs before putting it away.*]

YOUNG BOY: I saw you on TV. You that guy from TV? You that guy from TV? I saw you on TV!

MANNY [*making himself presentable*]: Yep, that's me. You got me.

YOUNG BOY: I could see your medal?

TYKEEN: You finally got that medal?

MANNY: Ty, where have you been?

YOUNG BOY: I could see your medal?

MANNY: All right, all right, young soldier. But first, I gotta see your salute. Stand tall, stand strong. Ten-hut! Very nice. At ease. Now, come close, cuz I only show it once.

[MANNY *opens his jacket showing his medal.*]

YOUNG BOY: Wow!

TYKEEN [*coming closer*]: Yo, Manny, that shit's tight. That's copper?

MANNY: Ty, some respect, please?

TYKEEN: Oh, my bad.

YOUNG BOY: Wow!

MANNY [*to* YOUNG BOY]: Now, young soldier, your mission—to gather all items needed to survive today's storm. Whatever your mom needs, one Hershey bar, one bag of nachos, one video game of choice, and two tubs of the best Italian ices this side of Mulberry. That is an order!

YOUNG BOY: Aye, aye, Captain!

[*The* YOUNG BOY *salutes and yells as he runs off:*]

Yo! This the guy from TV! This the guy from TV!

TYKEEN: Yo, you famous! I love that story about how you got that. You could tell it to me again?

MANNY: Ty, maybe some other day. I got a million things to do before it gets bad out here and . . .

TYKEEN: Pleeeeeeease.

MANNY: All right, but let's walk and talk.

TYKEEN: A'ight!

[TYKEEN *hands* MANNY *the joint.*]

MANNY: All right. [*Taking the joint to his lips and inhaling deeply*] So, the sun was setting on the horizon. It's freezing cold outside. I'm driving our Humvee down this narrow road. It's me, Brad Ferguson, and Mike O'Healey. All listening to Jane's Addiction. [*Singing*] *Comin' down the mountain!!!* I'm driving and singing at the top of my lungs when I see these three women waving. Three beautiful women.

TYKEEN: Yo, I like this story already.

MANNY: I slow down and one of them holds out her hand. It's bleeding. I pull over to help her. Careful. Always aware of these crazy nuts liable to do anything around here. And then she starts laughing. And then her girlfriend starts laughing. Then, her other girlfriend starts laughing. And I get this bad feeling in my gut. So, I steer the Humvee back down the road and I say "Let's get outta . . ." BOOM. And all I know is that our Humvee is flipping in the air in slow motion. Bullets are flying from God knows where. I look over at Brad and Mike. "BRACE!" then another BOOM. And our Humvee goes flipping in the air and it hits the ground—BOOM. BOOM. BOOM. And then and then . . .

TYKEEN: Loud silence.

MANNY: Yeah. The loudest silence ever. It's hard to figure out where we are. And my head is killing me. And on one side, I got my finger in a hole in Mike's chest to stop the blood. And on the other side I'm giving Brad mouth-to-mouth.

TYKEEN: Which was not easy to do because his breath stank!

MANNY: Yo, you remember that part!

TYKEEN: Yo, then what happened?

MANNY: Then another . . . BOOM! All three of us blown like forty feet into the middle of this dark river. Cold river. My head is pounding. And all I see was my life flashing before my eyes. Aisha's smile, Candi's laugh, Papí's farts. Communion at Our Lady of Sorrows, first day at Stuyvesant . . . And then I see her like a, I don't know what.

TYKEEN: Like a vision.

MANNY: Yeah, like a vision.

TYKEEN: Like an angel.

MANNY: Yeah, an angel.

TYKEEN: Was it a naked Taliban chick?

MANNY [*pausing*]: Do you remember me telling you about a naked Taliban chick?

TYKEEN: No, I just thought . . .

MANNY: There was no naked Taliban chick. There's never a naked Taliban chick. In any of my stories.

TYKEEN [*realizing*]: Oh yeah. That's true!

MANNY: Yeah. So, I see her, this vision, this angel. My mother. Pink light all around her, wings outstretched. She hands me three life jackets. One for me. One for Mike. One for shit-breath Brad. Except, these are not your standard life jackets. They are those bright-yellow kiddie floatie thingies.

TYKEEN: The ones for your arms?

MANNY: Yeah, the ones Papí taught all of us with at the Pitt Street pool. I get on my back, still with my finger in that hole in Mike's chest. And put Brad on top of Mike.

And my head is killing me. But, there's Mamí guiding me all the way. "Eswim!" She says, "Eswim! Eswim!" And I do Papí's famous one-armed backstroke all night long. They find us the next morning. Bullet to my head and nobody dead. And my faith in angels born again. Hallelujah!

TYKEEN: Hallelujah!

MANNY: Ha. Lle. Lu. Jah! A few months later, I got *this*. My Silver Star. I name her Doña Lola.

TYKEEN [*grabbing* MANNY *with pride*]: Not bad for a kid from the L.E.S.

[*They laugh.*]

MANNY: Let's go get this slice.

TYKEEN: Ooh, I feel so . . . so . . . patriotic.

MANNY: You look so . . . so . . . idiotic.

TYKEEN: Uuummmm, a slice with extra cheese with a Jamaican beef patty and cheese and a cheeseburger with fries and cheese doodles with a Coke and . . .

SCENE 5

[EVELYN *is at home.* CANDI *sleeps in her chair.* EVELYN *is meditating with her online class.*]

TEACHER [*online*]: OMMMMMM.

EVELYN: *OMMMMMMM.*

TEACHER [*online*]: Mmmm. And we open our eyes and we start our class today with a question. Probably the most important question to date. What made you go into the healing arts? Anyone? Anyone? Evelyn, can we start with you?

EVELYN: Um, I need a job.

TEACHER [*online*]: Aha. Is there *another* reason why you chose this path?

EVELYN: No, I just, you know, need a job. To pay the bills. Food on the table, that whole bit. I take care of my daughter full time, so I need something flexible around her schedule. She's fifteen. Sixteen next month. Teenagers! [*Chuckling*] AAAH!

[*Beat.*]

Four years ago she had what the doctors say is some form of a brain aneurysm, but they don't know for sure. And so she cannot speak or eat or, um, breathe on her own. Bathing her is a real trip. So, yeah.

[*Beat.*]

I was a conductor for the MTA. "Ladies and gentlemen, this is Times Square–Forty-Second Street. Transfer here for the A, C, E, N, Q, R, Two, Three, Seven, and Shuttle trains to Grand Central. Next stop Thirty-Fourth Street–Penn Station. Watch the closing doors." They used to tell me my voice was . . . nonethnic. [*Chuckling*] Now I'm just . . . here.

[*Beat.*]

Before this she was a star student. Straight As, honor roll, never missed a day of school. Wrote prize essays, got awards from the PAL and the mayor's office. She wants to be a congresswoman. I know when she told me, I was like, "Really? Seriously, Candi?" Then I secretly googled what Congress people do. I didn't know. I mean, do you know what a congresswoman really does? Oh, you do. Oh.

[*Lights change and we see* CANDI, *age ten, energetic, bright, and able bodied.*]

"Mamí, it's simple. A congresswoman is a person who has been appointed or elected and inducted into an official body called Congress, typically to represent a particular constituenceee in a legislassuure. That sounds like Latin. I'm gonna look it up . . . I want to help those to help themselves."

She is so smart. And she can only watch NY1. All day, every day. She says it keeps her brain from turning to mush.

[EVELYN *is lost in thought.*]

Mush.

[*Beat.*]

[*Again speaking as* CANDI, *age ten, and giving out pamphlets*] "Did you know that this part of the Lower East Side is one of the most underrepresented neighborhoods in all of Manhattan? We can't have that, people! I heard that when the towers came down, it took the media a million years to even report on the effects here. My mom works in the subways. She talks to me every day about the tiled glories of the Columbus Circle station, the modern art at Rockefeller, and the Renaissance architecsssure in some secret City

Hall station, while our own sad East Broadway stop is an eye sore, falling apart with every rumble of the F train. How many more tragedies do we have to go through before we rise up against the Man, I mean the system, I mean bad people? Maybe that man is the mayor, maybe he's your teacher, maybe he's Ronald McDonald beckoning you to a life of fast food and high blood pressure. Come on, *mi gente*, get up and make something out of yourselves! Take time to read the papers, watch the news. Get informational! Might I suggest New York 1, and for your Spanish-speaking families, NY1 Noticias? There's the City of Water Day every July. Tenement Talks on Orchard Street. The Nuyorican Poets Cafe, for crying out loud! I am Candace Lola Vega. Vote for me for fifth-grade class president. I am dedicated, kind, loyal, hardworking, liberal . . . conservative, and I speak Latin. We must want to strive for greatness! Or, we will DIE unknown, unseen, unheard!!!"

That's my Candi. She came out of the womb strong. Strong arms. Strong legs. Strong body. Papí taught her to swim, and she got the backstroke like [*snapping her fingers*] that.

[*Beat.*]

She's sleeping now. She's calm. You ask me why I got into the healing arts. My daughter has not been able to call me Mamí in forty-eight months and seven days and five hours. Doctors say she'll be like this for the rest of her life. But, I say she will be in Congress one day. Representative Candace Lola Vega from New York's District Twelve at your service. Helping those to help themselves!

TEACHER [*online*]: Beautiful, Evelyn. And Josephine, why did you go into the healing arts?

[*Lights shift.* EVELYN *is in her own world.*]

EVELYN: Oh Doña Lola, awaken your granddaughter, Candace. Awaken her, so she may live again!

[EVELYN *places her right hand above* CANDI's *head. The lights flicker off and on.* EVELYN *becomes* DOÑA LOLA *for a moment.* DOÑA LOLA *breathes heavily as if possessed, her right hand making circles above* CANDI's *head.* DOÑA LOLA *turns back into* EVELYN, *who looks at her hand with amazement.*]

Candi! Something's happening!!!

[*In an instant,* EVELYN *turns back into* DOÑA LOLA. *With eyes closed, she claps three times as she did in scene 1 and takes a deep breath. Then she opens her eyes and looks directly at the audience.*]

DOÑA LOLA: Do you remember?

[DOÑA LOLA *beckons to the audience to join her. She claps three more times. Inhale and exhale.*]

One more time!

[*With the audience members,* DOÑA LOLA *claps three times. Inhale and exhale.*]

Very good. Very good.

[*Eyes closed,* DOÑA LOLA *encircles the audience with healing energy. She then brings this energy to* CANDI. *She looks at* CANDI.]

Now, you feel good. *Gracia a Dios.* Thank You, God! Thank You, God. Thank You . . .

SCENE 6

[MOHAMMED's *corner store.* MOHAMMED, *the owner, listens to a popular Yemeni song while getting ready to close the store.*]

TYKEEN: Mohammed! *Assalamu alaikum!*

MOHAMMED: *Malakim Salaam! Kaif Al-Hal?* Mr. Clean Tykeen.

TYKEEN: Yo, you know Manny?

MOHAMMED: Ah yes, Manny. I remember you. The Lower East Side Hero! You are just back from . . . from . . . from . . . ?

MANNY: Ty, is it me, or is it really loud in here?

MOHAMMED: From . . . from . . . from

TYKEEN: Nah, Mohammed's deaf in one ear.

MANNY [*speaking louder*]: Can I play my dad's lotto?

MOHAMMED: From . . . from . . .

MANNY: Can I play my dad's lotto?

MOHAMMED [*lowering music*]: Ah, yes, gimme the numbers.

TYKEEN: Yo, Manny, thirsty? [*Opening the drink*] Taste this!

MANNY: I'm not drinking caffeine.

MOHAMMED: What are your numbers?

TYKEEN [*whispering*]: You just kicked some Arab ass and you're not even gonna try . . . ?

MOHAMMED: Numbers. Numbers. What are your numbers?

MANNY: All right, all right, hold on. Let me remember. [*Looking around*] Your son still work here? What was his name?

TYKEEN: . . . and you're not even gonna try this. You got soft on me!

MOHAMMED: Which son? Amir?

MANNY: No.

MOHAMMED: Abdul?

MANNY: No.

MOHAMMED: Hakeem.

MANNY: No.

MOHAMMED: John?

[*Beat.*]

MANNY: No.

MOHAMMED: Oh, Malik!

MANNY: Yeah, Malik. Where is he?

MOHAMMED: He went back home.

MANNY: Yeah? Why?

TYKEEN: Manny, you gotta try this. Come on. Taste like red Kool-Aid.

MANNY: That shit's poison, Ty. [*To* MOHAMMED] What's home?

TYKEEN: But, it's FDA approved.

MOHAMMED: What do you mean "What's home?"

MANNY: I mean what's home? Where's home? What's waiting for him at home? Who's waiting for him at home?

TYKEEN: Just one taste?

MANNY: All right, Ty! Damn! You always get what you want.

TYKEEN: What do that mean?

MOHAMMED: My son went back home to his family.

MANNY [*drinking*]: Yeah, I bet.

MOHAMMED: What does that mean?

MANNY: See, Ty, I'm smoking your smoke. I'm drinking your drink.

[MANNY *finishes the drink, drops it, and crushes the can with his foot.*]

MOHAMMED: No littering. Come on. Numbers, numbers, what are your numbers?

TYKEEN: I know his dad's numbers. One-one-six straight . . .

MANNY: How you know his numbers?

TYKEEN: He makes me play them sometime. No big . . .

MOHAMMED: What else? Numbers. Numbers. What are your numbers?

MANNY [*to* MOHAMMED]: Hold on, champ. [*To* TYKEEN] So, you're his son now?

TYKEEN: Man, we gotta get you that slice. Can't you eat one of them bialys?

MANNY: They're not for me.

TYKEEN: Lemme get a Jamaican beef patty with cheese . . .

MANNY: Are you his son now?

TYKEEN: Jamaican beef patty with cheese . . .

MANNY: Are you my *papí*'s son now? Answer me, soldier!!!

TYKEEN: Uh-oh. Here we go, everyone take cover. He's gonna blow.

MANNY: Is it possible to not start every sentence with a joke, Ty?

MOHAMMED: Come on! Numbers. Numbers. Or, take this outside.

MANNY: Take what outside? Fucking sheik telling me to take this outside.

MOHAMMED: Come on! Take this outside.

TYKEEN: Yo, Mohammed, pay this nigga no mind. He's trippin'.

MANNY [*angrily*]: Who you calling nigga, soldier! I'm Puerto Rican and I saved your life!

TYKEEN: See what I mean?

MOHAMMED [*turning off music*]: I have to close up. Take this outside.

MANNY [*to* TYKEEN]: Did you have to take her too, soldier? I was this close to marrying her, soldier. I was gonna come back and propose on the top of the Freedom Tower, soldier.

[*to* MOHAMMED]: Five-thirty-three straight two times, one-fifteen straight three times, four-one-one box, no, four-eleven combo. No! One, two, three. AAAAH!

[TYKEEN *tries to calm him down. He gives* MOHAMMED *Papi's Pick 3 lotto numbers while giving* MANNY *a reference for each number.*]

TYKEEN: Manny, zero-six-zero straight two times your house number, five-three-three straight two times your mom and dad's first exchange, one-one-five straight three times your mom's birthday, one-one-six straight twice Candi's birthday, and four-eleven combo three times the day your mom died.

MANNY [*in tears*]: Mamí died on April eleventh.

TYKEEN: Easter Sunday. I know. I was there. It's me, Manny. Your friend?

MANNY: Why did you have to take her, Ty? You know I love her.

TYKEEN: *Her?* Aisha? This about Aisha? It just happened. She didn't know if you were . . . Life goes on, Manny. Come on. It's just a girl. Toughen up.

[*Beat.*]

MANNY [*to* MOHAMMED, *with growing fury*]: Where is your son Malik?

MOHAMMED: Twenty-three ninety-two and then I have to close, my friends, come on.

MANNY: Where is your son Malik?

MOHAMMED: I told you he's back home. He is back home.

MANNY: And all those fucking cousins that used to work here?

MOHAMMED: They are back home.

MANNY: But, where is home, prick! Yemen? Saudi Arabia? Iran? Where is home? With a wife? Kids? Secretly planning and conniving with your cell? What is home? A building? A mansion? A hole in the mountains?

MOHAMMED [*proudly, but with fear in his heart*]: Yemen! Yemen! My home is Yemen!

MANNY [*pounding* MOHAMMED *in the chest*]: Thank you!!!

[*Beat.*]

That's all I wanted to know.

MOHAMMED [*holding his chest*]: I am old. I don't want trouble. I don't want trouble. I don't want . . .

MANNY [*throwing cans, bottles, chip dispensers, and candy boxes to the ground*]: This is my home. Manhattan Island is my home. New York City is my home. America is my home. Don't ever forget it.

MOHAMMED: I don't want trouble. I don't want trouble. I don't want . . .

[MANNY *bangs the store door open.*]

TYKEEN [*holding* PAPÍ's *lotto tickets*]: Yo, Manny! Where you going? Manny! Your numbers!

SCENE 7

[*Vega residence.*]

EVELYN [*looking out the window at the coming storm, with a rosary in her hand*]: *Santa María*, blessed is the fruit of thy womb, Jesus. *Santa María*, blessed is the fruit of thy womb, Jesus. *Santa María*, blessed is the fruit of thy womb, Jesus. Thank You for giving me Mamí, Papí, Manny, Mrs. Applebaum, my teachers, that snotty lady at Con Edison this morning, and Candi. My Candi. Every day, she is a miracle in my life. *Om namah shivaya.*

[CANDI *reacts.*]

EVELYN: Candi, guess what? If the lights go off today, we'll still be OK. Mamí was thinking! [*Pointing to generator*] Now, how do I turn it on?

[CANDI *chuckles.*]

You laughing at your *mamí*?

[EVELYN *finds the power button and turns the generator on. It is loud. Too loud. She turns it off.*]

Voilà!

[*She sees that* CANDI *is disturbed by the noise. She takes out her Tibetan singing bowl.*]

Santa María, Madre de Dios. They laugh at my singing bowl. They laugh at my crystals. They laugh at my candles. But, what do they know. Fire is the ultimate purifier. And, this, this is the room where magic is made. [*To* CANDI] When your grandma got sick, she closed the *botánica* for seven days and seven nights. She took out the whole bed and mattress and box spring *y todo* and she put it all out here. Then we prayed the *rosarios* together. *Santa María, Madre de Dios.* Papí sat on the bed with us, too, if you could believe it, not gambling, not drinking, not cheating—right here with his family. We prayed the rosary together for seven days and seven nights. Hail Mary. The candles, the incense. Full of grace. The rosaries, the *espíritus.* The magic in here would put that lucky tree out there to shame, Candi! Mamí would say . . .

DOÑA LOLA [*breathing and clapping with fury*]: *Santa María, Madre de Dios. Me ayuda.* Help me. Heal me. *Jesu Cristo. ¡Santa Teresita! ¡Santa Bárbara!* Help me. Heal me. *Chango. ¡Yemayá!* Help me. Heal me. *Jesu Cristo.*

EVELYN: It was a welcoming of all the saints and angels and gods and goddesses to come and hang out with us. Mamí had a direct connection. Then, Mamí started to shake.

DOÑA LOLA [*shaking*]: Out! Out! Out! *¡Sacúdete! ¡Sacúdete! ¡Pa fuera!*

EVELYN: Then she told us to open the door.

DOÑA LOLA: Get out, sickness! Get out, disease! *¡Pa fuera!*

EVELYN: Mrs. Applebaum came upstairs to see what all the commotion was about. Mamí didn't even see her. "Get out! Get out! *¡Pa fuera!*"

MRS. APPLEBAUM: I just wanted to borrow some sugar. I can see you're very busy. I'll come back later.

DOÑA LOLA: *¡Pa fuera!!!*

EVELYN: We watched her. Eyes peeled. We ate Ritz crackers. Body of Christ. We drank hot chocolate. Blood of Christ. I saw it with my own two eyes. *Om namah shivaya.* And then on that last day, that seventh day, Mamí rose up and said as loud as ever, "Cancer does not live here anymore. This is MY home. *¡Y YA!* Amen."

[DOÑA LOLA *claps three times then inhales and slowly exhales.*]

EVELYN [*composing herself*]: Then Mamí got up, put on her coat, walked back to her *botánica*, opened it up, and worked on anyone who came to her for healing. And they came from everywhere. Downtown, Harlem, New Jersey. Puerto Rico. Brazil. They came from Ohio and California. They came from Japan and Germany. All day every day. All for free. She didn't charge, not one cent. And that's how the great Doña Lola was healed. So they can laugh at me all they want. But they know. They know what happened right here. [*To* CANDI] Come on, Candi. Work with me. In the place where Doña Lola rose again.

[CANDI *reacts.*]

Open your eyes. Open your eyes.

[EVELYN's *and* DOÑA LOLA's *voices morph into underwater versions of themselves.*]

Open your eyes wide.

[CANDI *does.*]

Release your hands . . .

[CANDI *does.*]

Give yourself a deep breath in . . .

[CANDI *does.*]

And out . . .

[CANDI *does.*]

DOÑA LOLA: One more time . . .

EVELYN: One more in . . .

[CANDI *does.*]

And out . . .

[CANDI *does.*]

DOÑA LOLA: *Así eso.* You're swimming. Eswim. Eswim. Eswim.

EVELYN: Like you're swimming . . .

[CANDI's *breath starts out as a quiet whistle and gets louder and stronger with each breath.*]

DOÑA LOLA: *Eso es, Candi. Santa María, Madre de Dios. Santa María, Madre de Dios. Santa María, Madre de Dios. Jesu Cristo. Jesu Cristo.*

EVELYN: That's it, Candi. *Santa María.* You're doing it. *Madre de Dios,* breathing, Hail Mary on your own, hallowed be thy name, Candi, on your own . . .

[CANDI *takes a full deep breath in.* EVELYN*'s voice sounds clear again.*]

You're doing it, Eagle Standing Fish! You're doing it. Thank You, God. Thank You, God. Thank You . . .

[MANNY *bursts through the door.*]

MANNY: Evelyn, where's Papí? Hi, Candi.

EVELYN [*as if waking up*]: Manny, lower your voice. She's sensitive—

MANNY: —to the vibrations. Yeah, I know. I know. Toughen up, Candi! Where's Papí? PAPÍ!

EVELYN: He's on the phone. What's the matter?

MANNY: Papí! Papí, lemme talk to you.

PAPÍ: I'm on the phone with Migdalia.

MANNY: Man, fuck Migdalia!

EVELYN: Can you two lower your voices? She was breathing on her own.

MANNY: Ay, Ev. Wake up. She's gonna be cripple forever. Go back to the MTA and get a life.

PAPÍ [*entering*]: Don't talk like that to your sister, in front of Candi.

MANNY: And turn off that fucking TV. Turn it off!!! Or I will kill it. I will kill NY1. With a grin.

EVELYN: OK. OK. *Ave María*, Manny!

PAPÍ: *¿Pero qué pasó aquí?*

MANNY [*to* PAPÍ]: *¿Qué pasó? Qué pasó.* Well I am glad you asked *qué pasó.* So, I get my slice. It's delicious. And I'm about to walk home, when I decide to take Ludlow instead. Just for old times' sake. In this pouring rain. And I stop, and I am looking and I am looking. And I am looking. When were you gonna tell me about the *botánica*?

PAPÍ: Manny, calm down. You remember my egg foo yong?

MANNY: Yes, yes. I got everyone's fucking food and stuff. Can someone please tell me why there's a bank where Mamí's store used to be?

PAPÍ: These bags are so wet. You play my numbers?

MANNY: I forgot.

PAPÍ: You forgot? You forgot to play my numbers?!!

MANNY: Where's Ma's store?

PAPÍ: How you could forget to play my numbers? Now I gotta call Mohammed before he closes.

MANNY: Where is Ma's store! WHERE IS BOTÁNICA GUAYAMA???!

PAPÍ [*hushing* MANNY, *for* CANDI's *sake*]: I let it go, *coño*! I let it go. She never charged any of those people for healing. How was it supposed to last? In this city?!!! In the richest city . . .

MANNY: And where's the money I've been sending to pay the rent for it?

PAPÍ: With the landlord hounding me day in, day out. I don't know if you got the memo, but we're not the most desirable tenants in the Lower East Side anymore.

MANNY: I can only imagine who's getting that money, Papí.

PAPÍ: Manny, *dame un break-e*. How was it supposed to last?

MANNY: You're spending my money on your fucking *Price Is Right* girlfriend, aren't you? *¡Qué cojones, Papí!*

PAPÍ: Watch your mouth. You too tense. That's why you ain't got no woman in your life. Of course I spend it on Migdalia, *coño*!

[*Beat.*]

MANNY: Papí, you killed Mamí.

PAPí: You crazy? *¿Tú ta loco?*

MANNY: She was getting better and you killed her.

[*Beat.*]

PAPí: Did you smoke with that Tykeen?

MANNY: She healed herself from death. Her *botánica* was becoming famous . . . and then you went and killed her.

PAPí: *Ay Dios mío,* the last time I smoked with Tykeen, I woke up in some strange lady's bed with two dollars in my pocket, two teeth missing, and a dog fur in my mouth.

MANNY: She was only so strong.

PAPí: Manny, calm down. The woman had stage four cancer and never went back to get treated for it.

MANNY: First, it was that Jamaican lady from Cherry Street, then that Russian lady from Orchard, then that Filipino lady from Mott. Then Migdalia.

PAPí: You knew about Migdalia back then?

MANNY: Ugh, Evelyn, please . . .

EVELYN: Papí, we all knew about all of them. All the time.

MANNY: She died cuz of you, Papí. She died of a broken heart. In the end. Cuz of you.

[*Beat.*]

PAPÍ: No. No. No. Your mother, Doña Lola Vasquez Vega, was the love of my life. When I came back from over there, I didn't get a Purple Heart or a Silver Star. Or a whole page in the *Daily News* and a party. No one would even look me in my eye. Except for your *mamí. Mi negrita.* She was the love of my life. And I hurt her. Yes! But she was always at the *botánica* with everybody else but me. And I had to be a man.

[*Beat.*]

Mira, I killed for this country. And I did not kill men on Wall Street and rich *pendejos* in suits. And dictators and terrorists. I killed women. I killed chil . . . babies. And watched them die. And when I came back, from over there, none of these *sin vergüenzas* on Pike Street would even look me in my eye and call me a man. They would not even call me a man. I am a man, *carajo*! A man! And I killed the only *person* who ever loved me. Yes! I broke her heart. Again and again. I had to be a man! I had to be a man!

[*He pounds his forehead with disgust.*]

I had to be a man.

[PAPÍ *sobs.*]

[*Long pause.*]

EVELYN: Papí, I love you.

MANNY: I love you, too, Papí. Just, could you please stop . . . playing so many damn numbers?

PAPÍ: I stop, for good. Bad habit.

Maybe just one number. Five times each, and that's it. Or, two numbers, three times combo.

EVELYN: Can we . . . ?

PAPÍ: What is it, Evelyn?

EVELYN: Can we . . . ?

MANNY: What do you need, sis?

EVELYN: Can we all . . . take a deep breath in?

PAPÍ: Oh God, Evelyn, no.

MANNY: Not now, sis.

EVELYN: Please, can we just . . . ?

MANNY: Maybe later.

PAPÍ: This is not a good time, you know.

EVELYN: Please? For Candi? One breath, for Candi?

[*They look at* CANDI *and agree. Around her they inhale and exhale. Their exhales bring a great release.*]

MANNY: I'm sorry, Papí, for fucking this day up.

PAPÍ: What? No. No, *I* fucked this day up.

EVELYN: No, I feel like I fucked it up.

MANNY: No. I. Fucked. It. Up.

PAPÍ: OK, OK, we agree. We're a bunch of fuckups! Not Candi. She's the star.

MRS. APPLEBAUM [*at the door*]: Hello? It's Mrs. Applebaum.

PAPÍ: ¡*Ay Dios mío, esa viejita!*

MANNY: Pop, come on. It's Mrs. [*opening the door and hugging her tightly*] APPLEBAUM!

MRS. APPLEBAUM: Is that my boyfriend Manny?

MANNY: Is that my girlfriend Gloria? You ready for this hurricane?

MRS. APPLEBAUM: Hurricane? Ugh! I lived through the Renaissance. I saw you on TV. Very handsome. But what a shame about that Martin Luther King fella.

MANNY [clueless, but playing along]: I know, right? Such a loss?

MRS. APPLEBAUM: Tell me about it.

MANNY: Guess what I have for you, Mrs. Applebaum?

MRS. APPLEBAUM: My bialys?

MANNY: . . . and your pletzels. And your fire extinguisher!

MRS. APPLEBAUM: Did you . . . ?

MANNY: Take a moment to smell the pickles? Ha, I bought the pickles.

MRS. APPLEBAUM: Ugh, I hate pickles. They stink. You can keep them.

MANNY: Damn, Mrs. Applebaum!

MRS. APPLEBAUM: Gotta watch my stories. [To CANDI] Good-bye, my girl.

MANNY: Good-bye, Gloria.

MRS. APPLEBAUM: And, if I get swept away in the storm tonight, I'll die happy. Because I knew I was loved.

MANNY: Oh Gloria, you're not gonna die tonight. I would never let anything happen to my little lady.

[MRS. APPLEBAUM bats her eyelashes.]

MRS. APPLEBAUM: Well, welcome back home . . . to America!

MANNY: Be careful . . . walking down . . . the . . .

[*The lights flicker off and on again.*]

EVELYN: Manny, help me put Candi in the bath. Last time we didn't have water for ten days. *¡Y fó!*

PAPÍ: But, that's why we got that machine.

EVELYN: Yeah, Papí, don't touch it. It's very tricky.

PAPÍ: Prieta, let me for once be the man of the house.

[PAPÍ *walks up to* CANDI.]

Candi, I believe in you. I believe.

[CANDI *blinks three times.*]

Ah, she blink three time. She blink three time . . . Atsa lucky number zero-zero-three.

MANNY: All right, all right Papí, enough! Get her respirator. Candi, let me put you in the bath.

[MANNY *leaves, holding a chuckling* CANDI.]

[PAPÍ, *not far behind, places the respirator in the bathroom with* CANDI.]

PAPÍ: That's my Candi! [*Coming back to the living room*] Evelyn, high five?

EVELYN: OK. OK, first and last one for the day.

PAPÍ: *¡Así eso!* I'll drink to that!

[*The lights flicker off and on.*]

Just another relaxing day at the Vega residence.

[*The lights flicker off, then on, then off.*]

    ¡Punyeta! Where's my drink?

EVELYN: It's in your hand, Papí. Watch out for the candles.

PAPÍ: But let me do the generator.

EVELYN: No, not yet. Give it a few minutes. We'll get the lights back on.

[*The lights come back on.* MANNY *returns to the living room, closing the bathroom door behind him.*]

    See? Psychic! Is Candi OK?

MANNY: Yep! Got the water running. She was actually giggling a little.

EVELYN: Giggling? OK, let me get in there. She hates being alone for more than . . .

[*The lights shut off.*]

EVELYN: Manny? Could you turn on the generator?

MANNY: Where is it?

EVELYN: By the window.

[*He walks to the window in darkness. The wind gets stronger and stronger until, CRASH. It's the lucky tree outside, cracked and crashing through the window.*]

PAPÍ: *¡Coño!* Blow out these candles!

EVELYN: Manny, do the generator!

MANNY: It tipped over! Blow out these candles!

EVELYN: Let me get Candi out of the . . . The door is locked! The door is locked! Why is the door locked? Candi? Candi!

[*Part of the generator explodes. The candles set fire to the room. The room is engulfed in flames.*]

PAPÍ: *¡Ave María! ¡Dame el* fire extinguisher!

MANNY: We don't have it!

PAPÍ: What you mean we don't have it!

EVELYN: Manny, help me get Candi out of the . . . !

PAPÍ: Manny, help me!

EVELYN: Manny, help me!

PAPÍ: Manny!

EVELYN: Manny!

MANNY: Ev, hold on! I got you, Pop.

EVELYN [*speaking loudly yet calmly in* CANDI's *direction*]: Candi, don't be afraid. Keep breathing. We're coming to get you, Candi! Mamí's coming to get you! Mamí's coming, Candi. Keep breathing. Keep breathing . . . !!

[*Blackout.*]

SCENE 8

REPORTER [*voiceover*]: Welcome back to our twenty-four-hour coverage of Hurricane Dolores and the recovery and rescue efforts following its punishing blows. Firefighters in the Lower East Side battled a deadly five-alarm fire throughout the night during the storm's peak. The fire was apparently started by a gas generator on the fifth floor of a tenement walk-up. Witnesses say lightning struck an eighty-year-old oak tree in front of the apartment building, followed by a loud crash and explosion before the flames forced them to flee into the torrential rain and ninety-mile-per-hour wind. One of the lucky few to escape the building was a ninety-five-year-old Holocaust survivor who said her fire extinguisher saved her. Three bodies were later found in an apartment: an elderly man, a woman in her thirties, and a man whom authorities later identified as decorated U.S. Navy Seal Manuel Vega.

[*Beat. A spotlight slowly brightens on* CANDI.]

But, a teenage girl was found alive in the bathtub, reportedly *doing the backstroke.* Police have yet to identify her but say she has only spoken three words, quote, "Swim. Swim. Swim."

[*Beat.* CANDI *is mouthing the words "Swim, Swim, Swim."*]

Stay with us as we continue our coverage in the days ahead, and hopefully, with more stories of survivors, like this one . . .

[MAGIC MOMENT #5—CANDI *is doing the backstroke.*]

[*As* CANDI's *backstroke gets stronger, her hands meet in a loud clap. After another stroke, we hear a second. Then a third boisterous clap. Her last clap lifts her hands up in a revival position, eyes and arms up outstretched to the sky. She inhales forcefully. She exhales sweetly. Blackout.*]